The Little Book of Laughter

Over 100 Jokes, Riddles and Rhymes to Brighten Your Day

Compiled by Maureen Sangiorgio

Published by Waldorf Publishing
2140 Hall Johnson Road
#102-345
Grapevine, Texas 76051
www.WaldorfPublishing.com
The Little Book of Laughter
Over 100 Jokes, Riddles and Rhymes to Brighten Your Day
ISBN: 978-1-64255-776-3
Library of Congress Control Number: 2018901264
Copyright © 2018

All rights reserved. No part of this book may be reproduced or transmitted in any form or by any means whatsoever without express written permission from the author, except in the case of brief quotations embodied in critical articles and reviews. Please refer all pertinent questions to the publisher. All rights reserved. No part of this book may be reproduced or transmitted in any form or by any means, electronic or mechanical, including photocopying, recording, or by an information storage and retrieval system except by a reviewer who may quote brief passages in a review to be printed in a magazine or newspaper without permission in writing from the publisher.

Acknowledgements

The Editor does not claim to be the original author of the jokes, riddles, limericks, and one-liners contained in The Little Book of Laughter, and has made every effort to trace ownership of all copyrighted material. In case there is a question regarding the source of the jokes, we apologize for any error unconsciously made, and we will be happy to list attributions in any future editions of this book.

Table of Contents

Introduction 1
Chapter One: Blonde Jokes 4
Chapter Two: Married Couple Jokes............................ 12
Chapter Three: Mother-In-Law Jokes.......................... 22
Chapter Four: Office Jokes.. 36
Chapter Five: Sports Jokes... 50
Chapter Six: Riddles 56
Chapter Seven: Limericks 79
Chapter Eight: Funny One Liners................................ 87
Chapter Nine: Tickle Your Funny Bone 119
Chapter Ten: World's Funniest Jokes 159
Bibliography.. 171
Author Bio... 172

Introduction

William Thackeray once said, "*A good laugh is sunshine in the house.*" So true! And don't we all need to laugh more these days? According to a recent Harris Poll survey, only 33% of Americans surveyed said they were happy. The people who reported being the happiest were folks in high-income households (thanks Captain Obvious!), and those with a high school diploma or less.

So why are most Americans so blue? Survey researchers theorize people today are extremely busy -- working more hours with longer commute times than ever before. Survey respondents aged 65+ were the happiest -- retirees have more spare time to engage in hobbies and fun pastimes. The good news is most survey respondents reported feeling optimistic about the future.

So is Laughter *Really* The Best Medicine?

Actually . . . *YES!* According to the prestigious Mayo Clinic, whether you're reading a funny joke, or laughing at a hilarious sitcom, laughter is a terrific stress buster. Laughter actually stimulates physical changes in your body. Here's how:

- → Laughter enhances your intake of oxygen-rich air, stimulates your heart, lungs, and muscles, and increases mood-lifting endorphins.

- → Laughter activates your body's response to stress, creating a good, relaxed feeling.

- → Laughter helps your muscles relax and stimulates circulation, which can help reduce some of the physical symptoms of stress.

- → Laughter can help stimulate your immune system. Negative thoughts can eventually manifest into chemical reactions that can hamper the immune system. Conversely, positive thoughts can release neuropeptides that can help fight stress and serious illness.

- → Laughter can relieve pain. Preliminary research suggests having a good laugh can ease pain by causing the body to produce natural painkillers.

So sit back and get ready to laugh yourself silly!

Ok so who doesn't like a good "dumb blonde" joke? Well, if you think there's any truth in the old adage that blondes are dumber than others, the joke is on you! According to a recent study of over 10,000 Americans, white women who said their natural hair color was blonde had an average IQ score of 103, compared to 102 for those with brown hair, 101 for those with red hair, and 100 for those with black hair. The study was published in the journal Economics Bulletin.

A blonde walks into a store and asks the salesman, "How much for the T.V?" The salesperson says, "Madam we don't sell to blondes." The next day she colors her hair black then she goes back into the store and she asks again, "How much for that T.V?" The salesman says, "Madam we don't sell to blondes!" Upset her plan didn't work she said, "How do you know I'm a blonde?" The salesman replied, "It's not a T.V. -- it's a microwave!"

A blonde guy gets home early from work and hears strange noises coming from the bedroom. He rushes upstairs to find his wife naked on the bed, sweating and panting.
"What's up?" he asks.
"I'm having a heart attack!" cries the woman.

He rushes downstairs to grab the phone, but just as he is dialing, his 4-year old son comes up and says, "Daddy! Daddy! Uncle Ted's hiding in your wardrobe and he's got no clothes on!"

The guy slams the phone down and storms upstairs into the bedroom, past his screaming wife, and rips open the wardrobe door.

Sure enough, there is his brother, totally naked, cowering on the wardrobe floor.
"You idiot!" says the husband. "My wife is having a heart attack and you're running around with no clothes on scaring the kids!"

A blonde is on her honeymoon when her new husband asks,

"Baby am I your first?"

She replied,

"Why does everyone always ask me that? YES!"

A blonde, a brunette, and a redhead are all captured by a group of armed terrorists. The three women are told that they are going to be killed one at a time.

The men line up like a firing squad and the redhead is brought before them. The man in charge asks, "Do you have any last words before we kill you?" and the redhead answers, "Flood!" The men panic and run for high ground while the redhead gets away.

They figure out that they've been fooled and come back. After lining up they bring out the brunette. Again, the commander asks if the prisoner has any last words. The brunette answers, "Tornado!" When the men run for cover, she too gets away.

The blonde, watching the whole time, smirks. "I've got it covered," she thinks. "No problem." So, the firing squad brings her before them. "Have you any last words?" asks the commander. Grinning, the blonde instantly shouts, "Fire!"

A blonde, a brunette and a redhead were all working at the same office. They were secretly planning to sneak home early after their female boss goes home. The next day the boss leaves and they all sneak out early. The brunette and redhead had time to clean their houses and water their lawns, but when the blonde got home she saw her husband in bed with her boss. So, she sneaks back out without being seen. When they meet back at the office the brunette says, "Let's do this again tomorrow." The blonde said, "No way! I almost got caught!"

What does a blonde say when you ask her,

"What are the last two words of the national anthem?"

"Play ball!"

The Little Book of Laughter Maureen Sangiorgio

Chapter Two:
Married Couple Jokes

My parents were married for over fifty years when they passed, and had a wonderful marriage. Their personalities were complete opposites – my mom was very meek, mild, and shy. My dad was very outgoing, friendly, and funny. He had a terrific sense of humor. Whenever my mom would do or say something that he didn't agree with, he would always say, "Boy – when I said, 'I do,' I really did it!" I hope you enjoy these married couple jokes . . . .

One night, a torrential rain soaked South Louisiana. The next morning the resulting floodwaters came up about 6 feet into most of the homes there.

Mrs. Boudreaux was sitting on her roof with her neighbor, Mrs. Thibodaux, waiting for help to come.
Mrs. Thibodaux noticed a lone baseball cap floating near the house. Then she saw it float far out into the front yard, then float all the way back to the house, it kept floating away from the house, then back in.

Her curiosity got the best of her, so she asked Mrs. Boudreaux, "Do you see that baseball cap floating away from the house, then back again?"

Mrs. Boudreaux said, "Oh yes, that's my husband I told him he was going to cut the grass today come Hell or high water!"

While her husband was lying down, his wife removed his glasses. "You know, honey," she said sweetly, "Without your glasses you look like the same handsome young man I married."

"Honey," he replied with a grin, "Without my glasses, you still look pretty good too!"

A man is walking on a beach when he finds an old lamp. He gives it a rub, and out pops a genie.

"OK, you set me free," says the genie. "You have three wishes, but there is a stipulation. Whatever you wish for, your wife will get double."

What the genie doesn't know is this upset the man as he is going through a bitter divorce. The man thinks and says "OK, I'll have $1,000,000." "Done" says the genie, "and your wife has $2,000,000. What is your second wish??" "I want a large mansion." Again, the genie grants the wish and gives the man's wife a house twice as large. "And your final wish?" The man thought for a moment and said, "I want you to scare me half to death!"

There once was a little old man and woman who had been married happily for 75 years. They never kept anything from each other. But, the little old woman had a box in her closet which she told her husband not to look at. He respected her wishes and thought nothing of it.

One day the little old woman got very sick and her husband was afraid she was going to pass on. So, while she was lying in bed he brought her the box she had in the closet. "I think it's time you tell me what this is about," he said to her. He opened the box and found two handmade doilies and $20,000.

The woman started to explain, "My grandmother had a long and happy marriage and before I got married she told me that the secret to a good marriage was to not get mad with your husband. She told me whenever I was mad I should just go and make a doily."

The husband's eyes filled with tears. In their long marriage of 75 years his wife had only been mad at him twice! "And what is the $20,000 for?," he asked. "Oh, that's the money I got from selling all the doilies."

A wife went to the police station with her next-door neighbor to report that her husband was missing.

The policeman asked for a description.

She said, "He's 35 years old, 6 feet 4, has dark eyes, dark wavy hair, an athletic build, weighs 185 pounds, is soft-spoken, and is good to the children."

The next-door neighbor protested, "Your husband is 5 feet 4, chubby, bald, has a big mouth, and is mean to your children."

The wife replied, "Yes, but who wants HIM back?"

A young couple were on their honeymoon. The husband was sitting in the bathroom on the edge of the bathtub saying to himself, "Now how can I tell my wife that I've got really smelly feet and that my socks absolutely stink? I've managed to keep it from her while we were dating, but she's bound to find out sooner or later that my feet stink. Now how do I tell her?"

Meanwhile, the wife was sitting in the bed saying to herself, "Now how do I tell my husband that I've got really bad breath? I've been very lucky to keep it from him while we were courting, but as soon as he's lived with me for a week, he's bound to find out. Now how do I tell him gently?"

The husband finally plucks up enough courage to tell his wife and so he walks into the bedroom. He walks over to the bed, climbs over to his wife, puts his arm around her neck, moves his face very close to hers and says, "Darling, I've a confession to make."

And she says, "So have I, love."

To which he replies, "Don't tell me, you've eaten my socks."

I was enjoying the second week of a two-week vacation the same way I had enjoyed the first week, by doing as little as possible.

I ignored my wife's not-so-subtle hints about completing certain jobs around the house, but I didn't realize how much this bothered her until the clothes dryer refused to work, the iron shorted and the sewing machine motor burned out in the middle of a seam. The final straw came when she plugged in the vacuum cleaner and nothing happened.

She looked so stricken that I had to offer some consolation.

"That's okay, honey," I said. "You still have me."

She looked up at me with tears in her eyes. "Yes," she wailed, "but you don't work either!"

A guy goes to the supermarket and notices an attractive woman waving at him.

She says, "Hello."

He's rather taken aback because he can't place where he knows her from. So, he says, "Do you know me?"

To which she replies, "I think you're the father of one of my kids."

Now his mind travels back to the only time he has ever been unfaithful to his wife and says, "My God, are you the stripper from my bachelor party that I made love to on the pool table with all my buddies watching while your partner whipped my butt with wet celery?"

She looks into his eyes and says calmly, "No, I'm your son's teacher."

Mother-in-law jokes have been a standard of comedians for years, especially if they're male. But according to recent research by British psychologist Terri Apter, just the opposite is true. According to her book, "What Do You Want From Me?" the relationship between female in-laws can be much tenser than the one between a man and his wife's Mom. Apter discovered that more than 60% of women felt that friction with their husband's mother had caused them long-term stress. Compare that whopping figure to only 15% of men complained that their mothers-in-law caused them grief. So, the next time your mother-in-law is giving you a headache, reach for two aspirin and the following jokes!

The doorbell rang this morning. When I opened the door, there was my mother-in-law on the front step.

She said, "Can I stay here for a few days?"

I said, "Sure you can." And shut the door.

Kids out of control?

Here's a good tip: Display your mother-in-law's photo proudly above the fire. It will keep the kids away!

My mother-in-law is a well-balanced person.

She's got a chip on BOTH shoulders!

Q: What is a difference between "accident" and "tragedy"?
A: Suppose you are with the family and are beside a pool. You suddenly push your mother-in-law into the pool -- so it's an accident. If she could swim and gets out, in that case, it's a tragedy!

The newlywed wife said to her husband when he returned from work, "I have great news for you. Pretty soon, we're going to be three in this house instead of two." Her husband ran to her with a smile on his face and delight in his eyes. He was glowing of happiness and kissing his wife when she said, "I'm glad that you feel this way since tomorrow morning, my mother moves in with us."

Q: Do you know the punishment for bigamy?

A: Two mothers-in-law.

A man is driving with his wife at his side and his mother-in-law in the backseat. The women just won't leave him alone. His mother-in-law says, "You're driving too fast!" His wife says, "Stay more to the left." After ten mixed orders, the man turns to his wife and asks, "Who's driving this car – you or your mother?"

I was at a magic show, when after one particularly amazing trick, someone screamed out, "wow, how did you do that." "I would tell you," answered the magician predictably, "but then I'd have to kill you." After a moment's pause the same voice screamed out, "can you tell my mother in law?"

George went on a vacation to the Middle East with his family, including his mother-in-law. During their vacation in Jerusalem, George's mother-in-law died. With the death certificate in his hand, George went to the American Consulate Office to make arrangements to send the body back to the United States for a proper burial.

The Consul told George that to send the body back to the United States for burial is very, very expensive. It could cost him as much as $5,000.00. The Consul told him, in most cases the person responsible for the remains normally decides to bury the body here in Jerusalem. This would only cost him $150.00.

George thinks for some time and answers, "I don't care how much it will cost to send the body back, that's what I want to do." The Consul says, "You must have loved your mother-in-law very much considering the difference in price." "No, it's not that," says George. "You see, I know of a case many, many years ago of a man that was buried here in Jerusalem. On the third day he arose from the dead! I just can't take that chance!"

So, David is finally engaged, and is excited to show off his new bride. "Ma," he said to his mother, "I'm going to bring home three girls and I want you to guess which one is my fiancé." Sure enough twenty minutes later, David walks in the door with three girls following behind him.
"It's that one," said his mother, without blinking an eye.
"Holy cow," exclaimed David, "how in the world did you know it was her?"
"I just don't like her," she replied.

Office executive: "Sir, can I have a day off next week to visit my mother-in-law?"

Boss: "Certainly not!"

Office executive: "Thank you so much sir! I knew you would be understanding."

Someone going to work sees a large group of people walking. In the front of the group he sees a gentleman with a little dog, then a coffin, followed by the large crowd. Approaching the man with the dog he asks him, "What happened here, man?"

"My mother-in-law died," he said.

"How sad. If I may ask, how did she die?"

"My dog bit her…"

"You don't tell me! Could you lend him to me just for tonight?"

"Get in line!"

Chapter Four:
Office Jokes

If it's one thing I've learned in life, dear readers, it's that the people you work with can make or break a job. When you make your living in publishing the way I do, you're constantly under the stress of deadlines. But I've been fortunate to work with some of the most loyal, colorful, funny people that take the edge off the pressure, and have been a joy to work with. I wish the same for all of you . . . .

A jock and a geek are applying for the same job.
The boss said, "Boys, you need to take a test before you can get this job."

So, they took the test and the next day they came back to see who the boss chose. "Well," he said, "Both of you got the same score except I'm going to choose the geek."

The jock complained, "Don't you think that's prejudice or something?"

"Well," the boss said, "Let me tell you what happened. Both of your papers were right all the way through until the last question came up, and the geek answered 'I don't know,' and then when I looked at your paper, you answered, 'Me either'".

A Government Employee sits in his office and out of boredom, decides to see what's in his old filing cabinet. He pokes through the contents and comes across an old brass lamp. "This will look nice on my mantelpiece," he decides, and takes it home with him. While polishing the lamp, a genie appears and tells him he can grant him three wishes.

"I wish for an ice-cold diet Pepsi right now!"

POOF! He gets his Pepsi and drinks it.

Now that he can think more clearly, he states his second wish.

"I wish to be on an island where beautiful nymphomaniacs reside."

POOF! Suddenly he is on an island with gorgeous females eyeing him lustfully. He tells the genie his third and last wish:

"I wish I'd never have to work ever again."

POOF! He's back in his government office.

Sam walks into his boss's office and says "Sir, I'll be straight with you, I know the economy isn't great, but I have over three companies after me, and I would like to respectfully ask for a raise."

After a few minutes of haggling the boss finally agrees to a 5% raise, and Sam happily gets up to leave. "By the way," asks the boss, "Which three companies are after you?"

"The electric company, water company, and phone company!"

A young businessman had just started his own firm.
He rented a beautiful office and had it furnished with antiques. Sitting there, he saw a man come into the outer office. Hoping to look like a hot shot, the businessman picked up the phone and started to pretend he was working on a big, important business deal.
He threw huge figures around and made giant commitments. Finally, he hung up and asked the visitor, "Can I help you?" The man said, "Yeah, I've come to activate your phone lines."

One day a man goes to a pet shop to buy a parrot. The assistant takes the man to the parrot section and asks him to choose one.

The man asks, "How much is the yellow one?"

The assistant replies that it costs $2,000. The man is shocked and asks the assistant why it's so expensive. "This parrot is a very special one. He can type really fast."

"What about the green one?" the man asks. "He costs $5,000 because he can type, answer incoming phone calls and takes notes."

"What about the red one?" the man asks. The assistant says, "That one's $10,000."

Curious, the man asks, "What does *he* do?" The assistant says, "I don't know, but the other two call him boss."

An employee is getting to know her new co-workers when the topic of her last job comes up.

"Why did you leave that job?" asked one co-worker. "It was something my boss said," she replied.

"What did he say?" the co-worker quizzed.

"You're fired."

An employee goes to see his supervisor in the front office.
"Boss," he says, "we're doing some heavy house-cleaning at home tomorrow, and my wife needs me to help with the attic and the garage, moving and hauling stuff."
"We're short-handed," the boss replies. "I can't give you the day off."
"Thanks, boss," says the employee "I knew I could count on you!"

The sales chief, the HR chief, and the boss of a company are on their way to lunch when they stumble upon a beat up, but valuable looking brass container.

The sales chief picks it up and starts cleaning it with his handkerchief. Suddenly, a genie emerges out of a curtain of purple smoke. The genie is grateful to be set free, and offers them each a wish.

The HR chief is wide-eyed and ecstatic. She says, "I want to be living on a beautiful beach in Jamaica with a sailboat and enough money to make me happy for the rest of my life."

Poof! She disappears.

The sales chief says, "I want to be happily married to a wealthy supermodel with penthouses in New York, Paris, and Hong Kong."

Presto! He vanishes.

"And how about you?" asks the Genie, looking at the boss. The boss scowls and says, "I want both those idiots back in the office by 2 PM."

Moral of the Story: Always let your boss speak first.

A young executive is leaving the office late one evening, when he finds the CEO standing in front of a shredder with a piece of paper in his hand.

"Listen," said the CEO, "this is a very sensitive and important document here, and my secretary has gone for the night. Can you make this thing work for me?"

"Certainly," the young executive says. He turns the machine on, inserts the paper, and presses the start button.

"Excellent, excellent!" says the CEO as his paper disappears inside the machine. "I just need one copy."

A new manager spends a week at his new office with the manager he is replacing. On the last day, the departing manager tells him, "I have left three numbered envelopes in the desk drawer. Open an envelope if you encounter a crisis you can't solve."

Three months down the road there is major drama in the office and the manager feels very threatened by it all. He remembers the parting words of his predecessor and opens the first envelope. The message inside says "Blame your predecessor!" He does this and gets off the hook.

About half a year later, the company is experiencing a dip in sales, combined with serious product problems. The manager quickly opens the second envelope. The message read, "Reorganize!" He starts to reorganize and the company quickly rebounds.

Three months later, at his next crisis, he opens the third envelope. The message inside says "Prepare three envelopes."

Reaching the end of a job interview, a Human Resources Officer asks a young engineer fresh out of school about his salary expectations.

The engineer replies, "In the region of $125,000 a year, depending on the benefits package."

The interviewer inquires, "Well, what would you say to a package of five weeks' vacation, 14 paid holidays, full medical and dental, company matching retirement fund to 50% of salary, and a company car leased every two years, say, a red Corvette?"

The engineer sits up straight and says, "Wow! Are you kidding?" The interviewer replies, "Yeah, but you started it."

The owner of a company tells his employees:
"You worked very hard this year, therefore the company's profits increased dramatically. As a reward, I 'm giving everyone a check for $5,000."
Thrilled, the employees gather round and high five one another.
"And if you work with the same zeal next year, I'll sign those checks!"

Chapter Five:
Sports Jokes

I live in the Philadelphia area, and for the first time in franchise history, our beloved Philadelphia Eagles football team FINALLY won the Super Bowl! FINALLY! After 50+ years! There were many who would say the Eagles football team were a sports joke! Just goes to show you – don't ever give up on your dreams!

At one point during a game, the coach said to one of his young players, "Do you understand what cooperation is? What a team is?"

The little boy nodded in the affirmative.

"Do you understand that what matters is whether we win together as a team?"

The little boy nodded yes.

"So," the coach continued, "when a strike is called, or you're out at first, you don't argue or curse or attack the umpire. Do you understand all that?"

Again, the little boy nodded.

"Good, " said the coach, "now go over there and explain it to your mother."

There are two old guys in a park feeding birds -- Bob and Sam. They are big baseball fans, so they talk about baseball a lot.

Bob asked Sam, "I wonder if there is baseball in heaven?" Sam said he didn't know.

Two weeks later, Bob dies, so Sam is all alone feeding the birds. While he is sitting there, Sam hears Bob's voice saying, "Sam . . . Sam."

Sam says, "Bob is that you?"

Bob answers, "Yes, I have good news and bad news. "

Sam asked, "What's the good news?" Bob tells him there is baseball in heaven. Sam asked what the bad news is. Bob says, "You're pitching Friday."

A man is having breakfast when his wife comes on down and is very mad at him.

He asks why she's mad...

She tells him she found a piece of paper with the name MARILU on it.

He pauses and says, "Honey that is a tip on a horse that ran last week at the track."

Next morning his wife comes down extremely mad this time, and starts slapping him. He asks, "What now?"

"THE HORSE JUST CALLED YOU!!!" she screamed.

A little Bear is at his custody hearing. The judge asks the little bear whom he wants to live with.

Well, I don't want to live with Mamma bear, she beats me. And I do not want to live with Papa Bear, he beats me too.

The Judge asks little bear if he has any relatives whom he likes.

Little Bear says no. . . I want to live with the Chicago Bears, they don't beat anybody.

The Little Book of Laughter　　　　　　　　　　　　　　　　　Maureen Sangiorgio

Chapter Six:
Riddles

Perfect for both young and old, riddles are great for forcing someone to think. Studies show that most people only use about ten percent of their brain capacity in life. Put on your thinking cap and get ready to use up the other 90% trying to solve these riddles.

You're running a race and pass the person in 2nd place. What place are you in now?

Answer: You're in second place. You didn't pass the person in first.

Imagine you are in a dark room. How do you get out?

Answer: Stop imagining.

Who makes it but has no need of it.

Who buys it but has no use for it.

Who uses it but can neither see nor feel it.

What is it?

Answer: A coffin

You answer me, but I never ask you a question. What am I?

Answer: A telephone

What can travel around the world while staying in a corner?

Answer: A stamp

Johnny's mother had three children. The first was named April and the second was named May. What was the name of the third child?

Answer: Johnny

Some months have 30 days, and some months have 31 days. How many have 28?

Answer: All of them

What occurs once in every minute, twice in every moment, but never in a thousand years?

Answer: The letter M

If there are three apples and you take two away, how many apples do you have?

You took two apples, so you now have two of them.

What has no beginning, end, or middle?

Answer: A doughnut

There is a word and six letters it contains. Take one away and twelve is what remains. What word is it?

Answer: Dozens

If you have me, you want to share me. But if you share me, you no longer have me. What am I?

Answer: A secret

How much dirt is there in a hole that's four feet by five feet by six feet?

Answer: There is no dirt in a hole or it wouldn't be a hole.

Two girls were born to the same mother, on the same day, at the same time, in the same month and year and yet they're not twins. How can this be?

Answer: They're in a set of triplets

At night they come without being fetched. By day they are lost without being stolen. What are they?

Answer: The stars

What is so delicate that even saying its name will break it?

Answer: Silence

You throw away the outside and cook the inside. Then you eat the outside and throw away the inside. What did you eat?

Answer: An ear of corn

What word in the English Language is always spelled incorrectly?

Answer: Incorrectly

What goes up a chimney down but can't come down a chimney up?

Answer: An umbrella

What grows when it eats, but dies when it drinks?

Answer: Fire

The more it dries, the wetter it gets. What is it?

Answer: A towel

Chapter Seven:
Limericks

I miss my father-in-law, Dr. Frank Sangiorgio. He passed a few years ago. He was a man of the world! Very cultured, widely traveled, well-read, and highly intelligent. He was the one who turned me on to limericks. He could recite them at any time he wanted to make us all laugh at family get-togethers! Here are a few of our favorites, by the English poet Langford Reed . . .

I sat next to the Duchess at tea,
Distressed as a person could be,
Her rumblings abdominal
Were simply phenomenal –
And everyone thought it was me!

There was a young lass from Dundee,
Whose knowledge of French was, "Oui Oui,"
When they asked, "Parlez vous?"
She replied, "Same to you,"
A fine bit of fast repartee.

A girl being treated for hernia
Remarked to her doctor, "Goldernia,
When slicing my middle,
Be sure not to fiddle
With matters that do not conernya."

There once was a lady named Mabel
So ready, so willing, so able,
And so full of spice
She could name her own price,
Now Mabel's all wrapped up in sable.

There was a young lady of Florence,
Who for kissing professed great abhorrence;
But when she'd been kissed
And found what she'd missed,
She cried till the tears came in torrents.

An oyster from Kalamazoo
Confessed he was feeling quite blue,
"For," he said, "as a rule,
When the weather turns cool,
I invariably get in a stew!"

Chapter Eight:
Funny One Liners

Whether their sources are famous authors, philosophers, or even the Bible, check out these quotes about the importance of laughter . . .

Entire section of one-line quotes from the following source: www.laughteronlineuniversity.com

"Against the assault of laughter, nothing can stand."

Mark Twain

"Always laugh when you can. It's cheap medicine."

Lord Byron

"An optimist laughs to forget; a pessimist forgets to laugh."

Tom Nansbury

"As soap is to the body, so laughter is to the soul."

A Jewish Proverb

"Each of us has a spark of life inside us, and our highest endeavor ought to be to set off that spark in one another."

Kenny Ausubel

"Earth laughs in flowers."

Ralph Waldo Emerson

"From there to here, from here to there, funny things are everywhere."

Dr. Seuss

"Grim care, moroseness, and anxiety – all this rust of life ought to be scoured off by the oil of mirth. Mirth is God's medicine."

Henry Ward Beecher

"He deserves Paradise who makes his companions laugh."

Koran

"He that is of a merry heart has a continual feast."

Proverbs 15:15

"I commend mirth."

Ecclesiastes 8:15

"I have always felt that laughter in the face of reality is probably the finest sound there is and will last until the day when the game is called on account of darkness. In this world, a good time to laugh is any time you can."

Linda Ellerbee

"I have not seen anyone dying of laughter, but I know millions who are dying because they are not laughing."

Dr. Madan Kataria

"I will follow the upward road today; I will keep my face to the light. I will think high thoughts as I go my way; I will do what I know is right. I will look for the flowers by the side of the road; I will laugh and love and be strong. I will try to lighten another's load this day as I fare along."

Mary S. Edgar.

"If you don't learn to laugh at trouble, you won't have anything to laugh at when you're old."

Edgar Watson Howe

"If you are happy and people around you are not happy, they will not allow you to stay happy. Therefore, much of our happiness depends upon our ability to spread happiness around us."

Dr. Madan Kataria

"If you become silent after your laughter, one day you will hear God also laughing, you will hear the whole existence laughing — trees and stones and stars with you."

Osho

"If you don't learn to laugh at trouble, you won't have anything to laugh at when you're old."

Edgar Watson Howe

"If you have no tragedy, you have no comedy. Crying and laughing are the same emotion. If you laugh too hard, you cry. And vice versa."

Sid Caesar

"If you wish to glimpse inside a human soul and get to know the man, don't bother analyzing his ways of being silent, of talking, of weeping, or seeing how much he is moved by noble ideas; you'll get better results if you just watch him laugh. If he laughs well, he's a good man…All I claim to know is that laughter is the most reliable gauge of human nature."

Feodor Dostoyevsky

"If you would not be laughed at, be the first to laugh at yourself."

Benjamin Franklin

"It is bad to suppress laughter. It goes back down and spreads to your hips."

Fred Allen

"It's one thing to say, 'I don't fear death', but to laugh out loud somehow drives the idea home. It embodies our theology."

Rev. Laura Gentry

"Laugh at yourself first, before anyone else can."

Elsa Maxwell

"Laugh my friend, for laughter ignites a fire within the pit of your belly and awakens your being."

Stella & Blake

"Laughter connects you with people. It's almost impossible to maintain any kind of distance or any sense of social hierarchy when you're just howling with laughter. Laughter is a force for democracy."

John Cleese

"Laughter has no foreign accent."

Paul Lowney

"Laughter is a form of internal jogging. It moves your internal organs around. It enhances respiration. It is an igniter of great expectations."

Norman Cousins

"Laughter is a sense of proportion and a power of seeing yourself from the outside."

Zero Mostel

"Laughter is God's hand on the shoulder
of a troubled world."

Bettenell Huntznicker

Chapter Nine:
Tickle Your Funny Bone

Here are a plethora of creative ways to bring more laughter into your life, according to laughteruniversity.com.

Start smiling back at the shops and checkouts. A smile helps to strike up a random conversation that may lead to laughter as it is random.

Give genuine and generous compliments whenever you have the opportunity. We all are suckers for compliments, most of the obvious reaction is laughter.

Share your innermost Irrational fears with some friends you can trust. We all have Irrational and unreasonable fears, they do not have any rational basis, though they are there to be laughed at.

Get friends and/or family together to play a fun game such as charades, etc.

Start writing in your diary on a daily basis stories starting something like 'A funny thing happened today' writing the most routine and mundane things happened during the day.

Buy a ukulele and start learning via lessons and perform to friends and family in the opportunity.

Go to a charity fun run, there's normally some sort of dressing up involved. They are a great laugh.

Buy a few bags of balloons and fill your sitting room with at least 20 or 30 balloons, surprise yourself or someone in your family with a balloon filled room.

Host a funny hat party, any hat can be funny if you never wore one.

Watch comedy channels on TV.

Strike up a conversation with old ladies shopping at the markets, you can start by asking how you can tell the freshness of fish or which tomatoes are the best?

Watch old British comedy shows such as Monty Python and Benny Hill.

Buy at least five cheap dinner plates from charity shops and have a Greek style smashing time in your kitchen accompanied by Zorba the Greek music. Hum along the song as you are smashing the plates. You can also invite friends to a party where everyone brings a plate to smash.

Write a funny poem about an awkward issue or situation you are in and share it with a friend.

Ask a friend what was the last thing that made them laugh.

Create your own list or all the things that made you laugh and share with friends.

Turn the everyday mundane situations to a random short story and make sure that there is a miraculous end. Share the stories with friends.

Learn to recite a poem in another language or short piece in another language and recite to friends.

Have a roller-coaster ride or a night at the local circus.

While watching TV, repeat the conversations back trying to imitate accents, male and female voices.

Design your last day on earth before an alien invasion and live it to the max.

Have your caricature made by a street artist.

Pick nettles from your nearest park and make nettle soup, share with friends and family.

Spend a day watching your favorite comedy movies.

Go a local market and have a go at haggling.

Have a go at heavy swearing about something that annoyed you.

Make someone's best day ever, they don't necessarily need to know it.

Watch funny pet videos online. Dogs howling to music really cracks me up!

Have a pillow fight at home or at a party.

Every time you speak start your sentence with the same letter from the alphabet for one day. No one needs to know about it.

Develop a random tick for a day. For example, clear your throat every time before you speak.

Remember the children's games you used to play when you were a child? Why don't you play one or two with family and friends?

Write a list of all the things gone wrong the previous year and recite them to your friends or family.

Compile a list of your favorite jokes and learn them by heart. Tell them to your friends to see whether they'll laugh.

Buy a temporary hair dye and color your hair in a different color for a day. See how family and friends respond.

To lighten up your commute, tune the car radio to comedy channels instead of music or news.

Get all the junk mail you received and turn them into a paper balls. Have a paper fight with your family or with friends.
Over 100 Jokes, Riddles, and Rhymes to Brighten Your Day

Write limericks including names of your friends in them. Limericks are 5-line short poems where the first line rhymes with the second, third line with the fourth, and fifth line rhymes with the first line. Best and funniest limericks are the ones recited in the spur of the moment.

The Little Book of Laughter — Maureen Sangiorgio

Chapter Ten:
World's Funniest Jokes

So here we are at the last section of this book. I like to finish strong, so the last chapter is devoted to the world's funniest jokes, according to Oxford University researchers. Yes, these brilliant scientists actually took time out of their busy day to run a bunch of jokes past undergraduates at the London School of Economics. These jokes are the ones that received the highest ratings on the funny scale, so enjoy!

A guy is sitting at home when he hears a knock at the door. He opens the door and sees a snail on the porch. He picks up the snail and throws it as far as he can. Three years later there's a knock on the door. He opens it and sees the same snail. The snail says: 'What the hell was that all about?'

A genie, an idiot, and three guys are stranded on a desert island. They find a magic lantern containing a genie, who grants them each one wish. The first guy wishes he was off the island and back home. The second guy wishes the same. The third guy says, "I'm lonely. I wish my friends were back here."

It's the World Cup Final, and a man makes his way to his seat right next to the pitch. He sits down, noticing that the seat next to him is empty. He leans over and asks his neighbor if someone will be sitting there. 'No,' says the neighbor. 'The seat is empty.' 'This is incredible,' said the man. 'Who in their right mind would have a seat like this for the Final and not use it?' The neighbor says, 'Well actually the seat belongs to me. I was supposed to come with my wife, but she passed away. This is the first World Cup Final we haven't been to together since we got married.' 'Oh, I'm so sorry to hear that. That's terrible…But couldn't you find someone else, a friend, relative or even a neighbor to take her seat?' The man shakes his head. 'No,' he says. 'They're all at the funeral.'

A guy shows up late for work. The boss yells, 'You should've been here at 8.30!' He replies. 'Why? What happened at 8.30?'

Sid and Irv are business partners. They make a deal that whichever one dies first will contact the living one from the afterlife. So, Irv dies. Sid doesn't hear from him for about a year, figures there is no afterlife. Then one day he gets a call. It's Irv. 'So, there is an afterlife! What's it like?' Sid asks. 'Well, I sleep very late. I get up, have a big breakfast. Then I have sex, lots of sex. Then I go back to sleep, but I get up for lunch, have a big lunch. Have some more sex, take a nap. Huge dinner. More sex. Go to sleep and wake up the next day.' 'Oh, my God,' says Sid. 'So that's what heaven is like?' 'Oh no,' says Irv. 'I'm not in heaven. I'm a bear in Yellowstone Park.'

A guy dies and is sent to hell. Satan meets him, shows him doors to three rooms, and says he must choose one to spend eternity in. In the first room, people are standing in dirt up to their necks. The guy says, 'No, let me see the next room.' In the second room, people are standing in dirt up to their noses. Guy says no again. Finally, Satan opens the third room. People are standing with dirt up to their knees, drinking coffee and eating pastries. The guy says, 'I pick this room.' Satan says Ok and starts to leave, and the guy wades in and starts pouring some coffee. On the way out Satan yells, 'OK, coffee break's over. Everyone back on your heads!'

A young boy enters a barber shop and the barber whispers to his customer. 'This is the dumbest kid in the world. Watch while I prove it you.' The barber puts a dollar bill in one hand and two quarters in the other, then calls the boy over and asks, 'Which do you want, son?' The boy takes the quarters and leaves. 'What did I tell you?' said the barber. 'That kid never learns!' Later, when the customer leaves, he sees the same young boy coming out of the ice cream store. 'Hey, son! May I ask you a question? Why did you take the quarters instead of the dollar bill?' The boy licked his cone and replied, 'Because the day I take the dollar, the game is over!'

China has a population of a billion people. One billion. That means even if you're a one in a million kind of guy, there are still a thousand others exactly like you.

Two campers are walking through the woods when a huge brown bear suddenly appears in the clearing about 50 feet in front of them. The bear sees the campers and begins to head toward them. The first guy drops his backpack, digs out a pair of sneakers, and frantically begins to put them on. The second guy says, 'What are you doing? Sneakers won't help you outrun that bear.' 'I don't need to outrun the bear,' the first guy says. 'I just need to outrun you.'

A guy meets a sex worker in a bar.

She says, "This is your lucky night. I've got a special game for you. I'll do absolutely anything you want for $300 as long as you can say it in three words."

The guy replies, "Hey, why not?" He pulls his wallet out of his pocket and lays $300 on the bar, and says slowly, "Paint…my…house."

Bibliography

1. http://time.com/4871720/how-happy-are-americans/
2. https://www.mayoclinic.org
3. www.discovermagazine.com
4. www.jokesforfree.com
5. www.unijokes.com
6. www.content.time.com
7. https://albertaventure.com/2013/11/office-approved-jokes/
8. http://www.craveonline.com
9. Book: Lots of Limericks, edited by Louis Untermeyer
10. www.laughteronlineuniversity.com
11. http://metro.co.uk/2015/11/26/the-ten-funniest-jokes-ever-according-to-science-5527698/?ito=cbshare

Author Bio

Maureen Sangiorgio is an award-winning writer with over 20 years' experience writing for national print and online publications, websites, and blogs. Maureen has also been a contributing writer of over a dozen consumer health books, and has been a ghost-writer to several physicians. Maureen and her ever-growing family of fur-kids live in the Philadelphia suburb of Macungie, Pennsylvania.